Phantom Navigation

"Robert Frazier's collection *Phantom Navigation* offers a perfect synthesis of modernist poetry and science fiction. With deft, painterly strokes, Frazier's projective verse points our perceptions toward the mysteries of outer as well as inner space. Here, Swiftian witticism alternates with surrealist dream-chants; across a full range of poetic forms and feelings, the poet takes a deep inventory of the human heart at the intersection of infinities. This new collection puts a seal on Frazier's status as a grand master of SF poetry."
 — Andrew Joron

Phantom Navigation

Robert Frazier

Dark Regions Press
2012

acknowledgments

Works originally appeared in, or are scheduled to appear in: *2001: A Science Fiction Poetry Anthology, Asimov's Science Fiction, Amazing Stories, Dreams & Nightmares, Dwarf Stars Anthology, Grue, Ice River, Lady Churchill's Rosebud Wristlet, The Magazine of Fantasy & Science Fiction, The Magazine of Speculative Poetry, Mindsparks Anthology, Narcopolis and Other Poems, Pandora, The Pedestal Magazine, Poly, Portland Review, Publication of the Society for Literature and Science, Rhysling Anthology, Star*Line, Strange Horizons, Terminal Velocities,* and *Velocities Broadside #1*

"Matters of Size," "Comet 103P/Hartley,"
"Relic of the First Light," "Four Days in Nagasaki,"
and "The Modern Demeter"
are original to this volume

Cover by Margaret Fox
Interior collages by Robert Frazier
Text set in Adobe Minion

Copyright © 2012 by Robert Frazier
Cover: Copyright © 2012 by Margaret Fox

ISBN: 978-1-937128-25-8

Dark Regions New Poetry Series #2
Series Editor: Bruce Boston

First Edition
2012
All Rights Reserved

Dark Regions Press
P.O. Box 1264
Colusa, CA, 95932
www.darkregions.com

contents

Navigations

9   Phantom Navigation
10 Lament for Cyania
12 The Void Where Our Hearts Used to Be
13 True Night on the Generation Ship
14 Passengers: Limit Contact with the Volnarii
16 Piloting Alone Out There
18 Nadanadanada

Dark Futures

21 Wreck-Diving the Starship
24 Inside the Bubble Chamber
25 Where the First Backyard Spaceship Lifted Off
26 Presence of Ghost Doublets of Coded Neuronal Patterns
28 She's Her Mother's Daughter
29 And Drunk the Milk of Paradise
30 Snaking Toward New Albion
31 Mutability / Accessing the Imago
32 Dream Strata
34 These Dark Futures We Now Inhabit
38 When Will Time Unfold
39 He Who ...
40 Nekropoleis
42 Wereman
43 Attributes of Darkness
44 Macropolis

The Personals

47 The Alchemist Obsessed on Love
48 Bioluminescence / Night Surfing
49 Waiting for the Orionids
50 Crash Course in Lemon Physics
53 Fossil Light
54 Nightwalk

Frozen Moments

57   Robot Origami
58   The Obsessed Astronomer
60   Queen of the Lines
62   Friedrich August Kekule and the Ring
64   A Feel for the Heavens
66   The Starry Message to Galileo Galilei
68   The Flash Moments of Doc Edgerton
69   Matters of Size
70   Blood Tests
72   A Measure of Light
73   North 66 /Tapping the Juice
76   The Astronomer's Underlined Phrases ...

New Dissections

79   Seeking Out Lobbed-Finned Truths
80   Your Clone Returns Home
81   Bad Year for Astronauts
82   The Modern Demeter
83   Comet 103P/Hartley
84   Four Days in Nagasaki
86   Terraformations
87   Relic of the First Light

88   **Phantom Notes**

Navigations

PHANTOM NAVIGATION

No, no desire or true affection or special creation is left
unused in the half-light or full illusion of the navigator's watch
long-dead notions once considered mistaken are especially useful
to her impromptu lexicon of things immortal spectral and bright
such as ether that omnibus through which all cargoes must pass
such as the red imperatives which doppler her universes
spiked by harsh rays and worm-eaten with vacuities at the heart
or the gases scalped with one swift stroke from every doomed sun
or even the shadowy sinkholes and moons wrapped in cold airglow
so when entropic time makes of her a natural compass needle
and when she billows her sails then pure science clicks in place
which is more difficult to refute than engraved circuits
or the unlined continent of her translucent face
her process: thinking of her strings of phantom lovers left behind
those realtime flatlanders with short-fused smiles of magnesium
those fluid earthy embraces that meld soft as silicates so
temporary in form they migrate endlessly along glassine planes
those inamorata like exquisite egg-tempera portraits that tumble
and decay out the diaphanous vaulting of her skull
out where they're supposed to be a rudder for her nebulous quests
her course: a null warp out from the familiar passways to an
unmapped infinity where the final reaches the mute worlds expand
where their gravity shrouds unfurl with sonic enhancement
only to reveal whistlestops more fair more free than strange fruit
teaming with fresh potentials for love and their phantoms
whose residue will propel her further
will allow her to heat-seek on more target systems
thus adrift in this hinterland she feels that she's slowing
she's severing the umbilicus cleanly
nosing like a great ocean liner buoyed by darkness and
listening on all wave lengths for the ghostly pipings
of primal dust plus that flaring chaos of a new sun

LAMENT FOR CYANIA

We acknowledge the sacrifices
of a hole pilot ...

whose eyes have known
the black of a worm-sleep
so glacial and deep-running
that it colors them

whose mind burns
before thought flares nova

whose every twitch
and muscular action
seems like last inner
demons banished finally
to her exoskin
for expression

whose sight turns
in toward the core
of perception
before it goes snow blind

whose flesh stretches
into a membrane that
drifts over her

whose synapses percolate
with the memory of taste

whose lips dry
from every kiss
they have kissed

whose tongue falls leaden
and forgets
the dance steps of syllables
whose very forgetfulness
becomes a hallway
of blurred faces and
physics molten as glass

whose nose smells
the alien fields where dead
lay buried under red and gold

whose fear melts
from the warmth
of blood that ties
its binds tight

whose heart purifies
even as its pulse loses its way
when the worm hole constricts

whose labor for guidance
consumes them until they are
the labor itself
and then just
the guidance

whose skeleton
becomes hollow
with the original light

THE VOID WHERE OUR HEARTS USED TO BE

I've seen the best Void Runners of my generation
scarred, vectorless, tired of the emptiness
yet always craving the vastness

who were scrapped like fried jump-drive parts
who are still hooked on those stormy dynamos
those machineries of flight

who bay at the moons the suns the obscuring dust
waiting waiting to be transfixed and spread far
like passengers cryosealed upon a table

and when the change comes
the true weight of the multitude of lives
we have lived and burned will balance to zero

when the change comes
our Klein bottle souls will reinvert
make revisions to the vain yearnings we contain

and, yes, when the change truly comes
the oxygenating machines in our chests
will shiver in blue-shifted beats

charting us back from all the far neutopias
bridging the void the deserted streets
where our torn-out hearts used to be

TRUE NIGHT ABOARD THE GENERATION SHIP

An artificial blue of sky gives way to
the purple dark of Sun Ra's robes

emblazoned with glassy scintillae
a spill of ghost notes

trilling out & out
the silvery horn of Eternal Now

& we are in the black again
until the cyclical days flare their lights

hearings snatches of "Take the A-Train"
down the corridors through the airlocks

thrumming along the ship's exoskeleton
crossing plains of solar dust & nothingness

we must embrace whatever
solace we might find

whatever voices we might hear

PASSENGERS: LIMIT CONTACT WITH THE VOLNARII

1.
age is something the Volnarii wear well
and shed like a big cheap jumpsuit
note: slippery when wet

2.
you don't need a tongue to speak volna
just a sharp mind
they'll read it for you

3.
though slush sluices void-cold
through the many-chambered autopilot
within their hearts
don't *feel* the Volnarii are shiftless
they'll feel it too

4.
they were spliced out of your rib codes
to be the Charon boatmen of void cargo
the shift-meisters of n-space
think courteous
or consider a Thomasian "neuro-veil"

5.
you greet one by cupping hands and blowing
across the void you've created
but if unthinkingly you suck a breath
or forbid cough while in this posture
you're speared meat

6.
to gesture good luck
invert the cup and whistle
they'll pop the polyp-fingered replies
they use for the telepathically-challenged

7.
and never never underestimate a Volnar
add an extra kiloton to the ship's manifest
wear a full-body splash guard
give it wide berth

PILOTING ALONE OUT THERE

is like cave diving in the tropics
while everyone is asleep in stasis
you swim your ship
from the charted star clusters and
their warm bright light
toward the cooler blacker depths
you have only a small node of technology
a mere motherchip like a lamp to guide you

there is a time
when you can't tell where you came from
from where you are going
and you wonder if it is possible
to chart a way back to Earth
by the tiny flashes of physics
that paint these walls about you

and when you enter an unmapped passage
your own propulsion
the way it stretches time
seems to work against you
kicking up dark stellar matter
that confuses your sensors
you begin to doubt yourself
feeling as truly blind as the white shrimp
that scuttles in the lightless regions
of a deep ocean cave

it is only when familiar stars
begin to show on your screens
that you rise
on a current stirring in your heart
on its bubbles of relief and yearning

at last you breach the solar system
slide into the assigned orbit
and stare down at her
your world
the scarred green-brown barrens
of the Canadian Shield
the soft blue eye of a tropical storm
over the Indian Ocean
the sun glittering across the bay
of Rio de Janeiro
the golden canyons and mountains
your great grandmother called her Arizona

a voice hails you on the comm
no one you knew is left alive down there
but it is all familiar
all your family welcoming you
in a single 'hello'

you say with an exhale "we made it"
you think
will I ever leave again

NADANADANADA

Dispossess me of all heavenly preconceptions
about the friendly nature of the stars
yes all that ethereal and saccharine crap
on the glory hallelujahs of space travel
about how its desolate beauty touches the soul
because if it ever truly did
well ... kiss your ass good-bye
we're talking more than Eliot's wasteland here
more barren than Australia's dead heart
I mean a place whose architecture whose source codes
are written in the real cold equations
we're talking the absolute of absolute zero
nyetnyetnyetnyetnyet
the Big Harsh
so spare me
it's breathtaking if you're in orbit
or were cavorting on the Moon
during the grand Apollos
but years or generations adrift in a ship
absolutely
nada

Dark Futures

WRECK-DIVING THE STARSHIP

> "Of those who arose from a frozen sleep and fought their way toward the ocean's surface, toward the future on this distant world, only the strongest persevered. Our ancestors were forged diamond-hard, tested by extreme, chosen by fate, yet prepared only in their hearts. We owe them our reverence."
> — *Book of the Original Survivors*, 2/17

1.
things that cannot happen should not happen
    yet there my daughter swims into the glow of my diving lamps
    I imagine temporal anomalies or some deepwater cold equation

for Mira seems more palpable than the daily quanta of minutes
    since I saw her life swept away so many summers ago
    flung by the currents that often haunt the wreck of *Homeseeker*

but how can this happen ... let me shift back to this morning
    when I awoke in quarters breathing the familiar perfume of fear
    of sea air and exhaust and the sweat of restless salvage divers

2.
sunrise and six of us set a plan for reaching
    the less plundered decks by reverse-tracing a path
    that the ship's passengers once made to freedom

first I checked my blends then pony tanks then the holomaps
    dive prep is crucial when your jury-rigged space suit
    can balloon suddenly and lift you to glorious embolism

3.
two klicks out two hundred meters down
    off these alien shores colonized by our unwilling ancestors
    every one of us felt the vast presence of the ship

after two plateaus the descent opened up to a rocky shelf
    her main section lay beside a precipice that dropped to nothing
    I imagined an immense beast at rest in its foreign boneyard

the ship had lost its integrity and its raptor-like shape
    obscured by whiptail kelp and a massive school of butterfins
    that poured from a hull breech like crime scene tape

we swam into an inky dark cut only by our blue visor lights
    started along rope-marked passages we call the Trail of Hearts
        illuminating skeletons embalmed in weedy suits and

spagettied cables and knife-edged bulkheads and docking stations
    sealed forever from space all the realities of a shattered lifeboat
    plus the myths that have crusted about her and clouded reason

4.
one: she is our true mother a holiness calling us back to
    the frosty chambers where she'd suspended us for centuries
    two: she is merely ill-fated and curses all who dive her

three: a theorem I found unsettling but ultimately worthy
    Homeseeker is the embodiment of death transformed
    a malevolence still active still cogitating still in control

nonetheless we'd come here to exorcise such sentiments
    and dive her for her last useable bits of hard- and software
    to rend forever the clockwork of her immense arcology

5.
the trail zig-zagged from the hull breach
    deep into the central axis and every step of it
    a dizzying plunge punctuated by breaks to reset our ropes

when a hard current slammed into me sending me tumbling
    I passed rapidly through alternating light and dark
    and I felt as if the fabric of my being shifted

as if time rewound in the direction ahead
    the hypnotic possibilities seemed suspect
    riddled with as many ominous factors as bright ones

another slashing current carried me past flooded atriums
    then fatally far into the ship into her Mysterious Core
    the holy grail of ship historians and wreck salvors alike

6.
as I rebooted my lamps the Core stirred with riotous color
    all the sea plants and small animals
    so like yet unlike Earth's

never before reached and thusly unknowable unsafe
    the huge cryocenter seemed domed with real atmosphere
    I closed my air valve popped my helmet and

took the chance that could restore my chances at surviving
    I found warm mists and a ceiling like daybreak
    winking with clusters of organic phosphorescence

and there treading in green shallows was my dearest Mira
    a memory reborn only she was not the girl I lost not quite
    but a complex form whose physiology appeared attenuated

whose very phylogeny seemed to have diverged
    on a track toward a lithe and compact simulacrum
    arm-like appendages and the gilled head of a woman

I invoked her name knowing I was senseless disoriented
    then its/her eyes fixed on mine and spoke the single word
    that could pierce my grief-hardened heart ... *father*

every cell in my chest blackened burned hot
    I was truly lost yet I'd found the miraculous
    and perhaps a proof for the existence of angels

Postlude

its been hours in this incubator or perhaps a day
    a thin microbial caul films my suit and I brush it off
    and reassess my predicament in sharper relief

chalk one up for the theory that *Homeseeker* still hums
    that some trickle charge allows the ship its brain
    and chalk one also for the primacy of the mother ship

however scratch the theory that her luck is bad
    for pure luck has left this all undisturbed for years
    question: was it my almost-Mira or the ship itself

that sent me reeling and shipwrecked me here
    just another lost traveler
    finally seeking home

INSIDE THE BUBBLE CHAMBER

It's enough for a painful deportation
when protons embrace, match force,
and, like lovers, lock in a death
spiral for their duration on skates.
They decay brilliantly—through divorce—
fashioning curves of cold
breath on light-sensitive glass plates.
But for those who prefer less expedient
passions, this particle minute is hardly sufficient.

WHERE THE FIRST BACKYARD STARSHIP LIFTED OFF

Velocity Street ran next to the immense parking lot
of an IGA store and beyond that along a stretch
where half the meter poles were decapitated
stood rows of abandoned welfare tenements
a Pentecostal church and a blackened brick hotel
that kept a commons room with faded velvet
wallpaper and Space Cowboy still on the juke
we're talking inner suburbia gone to weeds
streetlights with no more wattage than a bug lamp
yet this was a place that Midwestern kids escaped to
far from potluck socials and the putting by of preserves
far removed from the slow burn of their futures
under the transmission cowling of a combine tractor
they found work at the NASA labs shared apartments
married saved for veneered furniture took a loan
for a second station wagon with a trailer hitch
popped out a few kids read up on warp engine science
and talked and talked on weekends about leaving
the Heartland for a place where the universe
whispered its mysteries in a primary hue

PRESENCE OF GHOST DOUBLETS OF CODED NEURONAL PATTERNS:
Relation to Synaptic Memory Storage

Key Words: code; trigger; recognition

Abstract
After the brainwipe takes
after his skull blanches inside to a pure chaos
there are only artificial means
only the neuro-stims and psychoactives
weak surrogates for those last years
Toumani cannot recognize

Methods
They unleash him at dusk
without ID tag without himself
an act of political vengeance

Discussion
Toumani wanders the African marketplace
of red and yellow fruit the size of hand grenades
squash shaped like truck bombs
he shows no recognition
griots celebrate, pluck their kora music
nagging at him with voices of tradition
he ranges into the rubbish-strewn alleys beyond
witches, fallen tribal chiefs, drug dens, safe houses
no recognition
and sure, he owns his freedom now
he can use any bathroom, any train seat, any door
yet in conclusion, realize this
the trigger chip lodged in his brain stem
waits to unleash a miniature Armageddon
awaits that cry of revolution to trip the light
that sign of one man / one vote
a moment of recognition

Appendix A
Drugged, his best refuge is into the ghost doublets
shades of old coded memories
neuronal residues
where faces Toumani strains to apprehend
loom black and friendly and vital and
nearly recognizable

SHE'S HER MOTHER'S DAUGHTER

There are no memories of a past life for her,
no such transference in the clonal processes,
just a kind of presence
faint as finger prints,
as fractures in the lunar crust.

Her face cuts a profile in holography
as familiar as her origin-mother's, and as
commanding, like that in the last grainy vids
downloaded from the Giant Orientale basin,
astonished eyes staring into the wall breech.

Her body casts the same willowy shadow,
stitched along the circular bottom
of the colony's grav pool,
black as solar panels during eclipse,
capable of sudden power.

And, too, there is this:
her irises open the same airlocks.

AND DRUNK THE MILK OF PARADISE

Down in the factory warrens of free Mars
Where the wars for independence are waged
With daily flash raids and midnight marauding
Lowly ice sellers live in seething turmoil

Here and there smart bombs carve dead pockets
Sudden amputations to key conduits and caves
Even more insidious are those subtle infidelities
The nano-driven retouches to reality

Rigging condensers from scrap and salvage
Juice-jacking off the power grid these vendors
Remap their peddling routes and push on to supply
The cold necessities of water for colonial life

The oldest the mama-san of ice mongers
Spends days within a bright tangle of fiber optics
And divines the shifting data floes
For miracles of revolutionary device

By night she sleeps beneath an ammonia haze
Dreaming of a plain where sweet dustless breezes
Blow constant as the whine of O^2 expellers and
Sacred rivers again run through rouge red rock

SNAKING TOWARD NEW ALBION

When technology is exhausted unable to cope
with dysfunction and decaying data nets
the light draining from fiberoptical walls
dying in vast hexahedronal cities of glass

Cycles within cycles within cycles will end
and we'll go nomadic lose all family ties
as the global village chooses anonymity
cloned in the likeness of a composite man

Then our voices will blend like bees' wings
into a blur of illumination a fused note
piping in choral crescendos to be released
to be swept up in the daily armageddon

Faces will become forgotten as minds are
fleshy notes carrying no charge or valence
save the shifting ethers within our eyes
those amber nebulae of emotional fire

If that fire too succumbs to reiteration and
the nine trillion names of love are spoken
then you and I will queue abiogenetically
grabbing for new converts as we huddle

Fused like paper dolls at the hip we'll
stretch between cities chained in ribbons
that adhere and splice and ceaselessly mimic
the gene maps to a lofted spontaneous being

If so transported you see me naked and bound
accept this as an incision of Time's razor
this simpler solution and twine quietly by
toward the darkening perfectly-curving horizon

MUTABILITY / ACCESSING THE IMAGO

becoming primordial or primal
or merely primes

now capable of a nightly pupal
state mankind devolves unrhymes melts

something dark and espresso-thick
with nucleic acids

form reduced to a vestigial
imprint reduced to an i-

deal the base corporeal
nine billion names seem insufficient

beyond recombinant here we're talking re-
stringing the helices

when all kinds are truly possible
can there be any sense of
kind

DREAM STRATA

1.
Incorporeal States

locked in place
the bodiless body glides
a foot over silken sheets
it glows internally with white
fibers of silken fire
from without it appears empty
begins to dissipate onto its space
a decompressed gas
a flowing window pane
until a sudden noise intrudes
shatters the glass of silence

2.
The Sensual Incubus

Each cerebral nuance too knowable
each bit of cellular data shouted
we feed to each other by dissections
and self-replications of the moment
and when our nipples touch we blank out
synapses rapid-firing like spark plugs
an agony that diminishes slowly
gridded in breathless echoes until
breath itself is a tactile landscape

3.
Transmigration

In the instant of rebirth we shudder
as does a rocket achieving escape velocity
and balloon above our waxen corpses
we see breath still fibrulating
upon the shrunken lips far below
eyelids jump like digits in liquid crystal
flesh leavened with solarized light
yet when the detachment is final
as the cut of an umbilicus
our vision wavers with imperfections
our blind thoughts set adrift
heat-seeking for the after-death
like viruses in search of habitable worlds
and their freshly minted vessels
as yet untitled

THESE DARK FUTURES WE NOW INHABIT

Night Vision

Once they put the kid no longer a kid
on an IV needle in the dim little vet hospital,
he slides toward a drowsy oblivion.
He rests knowing that ins and outs
of fluids control his balance, yet
he thinks of voiding spotty samples
for their bottles and test tubes.
Another pound lost, pissed away,
he doesn't care much about. But
when it's blood he loses, blood he's
preserved for a family never-to-be, that
preserves the salinity of primordial oceans,
then he feels confused, a little lost.
Only it becomes worse when he sweats
a trickle of pink and coughs phlegm.
Clips in muted grays begin to flicker
to life, ratchet through his skull.
Silhouettes through an infrared scope.
The crosshairs slowly zoom in.
He watches how he battered a mama-san
until his hands slicked with darkness.
How he tortured a VC with swamp water,
letting madness spread like the black
moisture beading the boy's face.
How his vomit browned from Agent Orange.
He struggles suddenly to hold on
and return to the cancer ward.
Exhales, tries to fill his lungs.
His breath becomes a red mist
obscuring the future.

An Unborn Girl Sees In The Dark Womb

Her father tugs his flowery trunks
up over his pink belly roll and tries
to get her mother to play frisbee.
As he chides her, he scratches sand in
hairs surrounding his womanly breasts.
Her mother looks up from her love novel
and sighs, a tire goes flat in her chest.
Her mother stands with her tanned legs—
jogged to streamlined perfection—
and thinks about surgery and her MASH unit
at Quang Tri and says she'd rather swim.

With her eyes closed, the girl buoys against the
gravitational pull, is carried along.
Her mother slips into the cleansing waves,
but the girl is flushed with impurity.
Death and dismembered images stain her.

She must daydream inside the embryonic heat
that hums between her brain halves.
She imagines the sun cooking through
the thin wrap of her amniotic fluid,
steaming her marrow to soft paste,
blanching the bones white as
the shells of arks or angelwings.
The buttery rays, the hard spectrums
cleanse her of impurities.
When she develops adult muscles and fat,
they will be screened out
Without sun, little granules will collect
in her tissues, engorge wiith shadow,
grow to the size of pomegranate seeds.
Without sun, she will be seduced

by the plodding, brain-slowing days
of easy meals and radiating televisions.

As the sun lifts her sunbathing mother,
the girl chameleons to the color of sand.
her skin glows like froth on a wave.
The heat shines through her skull
and transforms the beach
into a dimension of dry, actinic light.
She is pinned there, rigid.

Then she turns her head against
the sun's pressures with every fiber
of her being still left to her, still somewhere.
Her parents are gone, the beach is gone.
She is a featureless lump quivering
along the long and short waves
of the invisible universe.
She is pure, yes, and
awaiting the death
of birth.

Shadowtalk

He's aging, a survivor by default,
accustomed to the noise and heat of day,
when life and the heartbeat quicken,
or the wind blows vibrant as a flute.
Yet he finds its quiet refuge too short.

At night his pulse ebbs low in his chest as
the dampening bellows of a water buffalo.
He remembers the mud-dark vowels of shadow
as they plot against light, and he attunes to
their jungle sibilance scraping in his head.
The sergeant dribbling away in a cancer ward.
The fetus fighting off her mother's black memories.
They all visit him over and over.
Listen! There's talk of surprise eclipses.
Even the moon is a stark affront.
In league with clouds, they conjure
the stars to sputter, dim and wick out
under their thick waxen assault of darkness.
Listen! In the rectangles under his bed,
whispers spin curses into dust balls
and argue on devices to frag his eyesight.

In the moment the candle flares,
it briefly silences his unsilenceable scream.
It opens the light at the top of the well.
It unnames the name of a gone war.

WHEN WILL TIME UNFOLD

when no language utters mystery
not even the 0-1-0 code of matter unraveled

when no codes not even that of fringeware
are things incorruptible

when data corruption is the only generator
of new physics

when unbound physical event
streams through a neural net of purest tao

when neurons release
the Man-cipher node to node

when nodes piggyback on knowbot searches
or skirt loopy feedbacks of flame

when pure love comes flaming
down the angel bandwidths

when approaching the neoangelic becomes
an utterance of the mysterious

HE WHO ...

stands at the wall of remembrance and screams black fire
he whose ego swims in emptiness like the larvae of galaxies
he who haunts the very spaces between spaces themselves
he whose body is hurled by virgins from cliffs of chalk
he who levitates on physical fever then collapses from within
he whose thoughts are as webbed as cracks in a windshield
he who sits on the throne of twilight where no man can sit
he whose dreams writhe with the pure white static of a junkie's
he who walks through the burnt forest and utters silence
he whose shadow dies in a diffraction of the light
he who sleeps in sea foam frozen upon dark sand
he whose dry soul must drink its pint of wet
he who refuses to stand free
refuses all dissuasions
refuses to stop
he is the one you must trust
when your time comes
he who waits
he who refuses to
wait

NEKROPOLEIS
The White Cities of New Orleans

In these cities of decay and bright blue sky the dead pace forever
because their bones were interred above ground for you to disturb

bones made soft when the river backed up past Basin Street
or fired brittle when conflagrations swept above the Vieux Carre

such restless ones have been trodden by the early French
by ambitious Spaniards and then the iniquities of self-rule

the history of their sins is wrought in immortelles
woven into prayers of wire and beadwork and light

on All Saints' Day you hear them drumming through the earth
with their hearts of granite or wings carved in white marble

in the black alleys between tombs their disembodied voices
conjure spells with Dominican and Haitian accents

and down among the rusted fences of St. Louis One
the shade of a mulatto woman tries to grant them peace

but her own vault is chalked everywhere with signs of the X
you hear the wind keen its harsh vowels above her ledger slab

so beware Mama Laveau has the power of night over all
you who don't wear a dime on a chain around your neck

you with only flake or Mexican brown for philtres
who spit on the wrong side of a shadow

all you who pump Armageddon through your heads
with a taste for violence on your tongue

and a sheet of cold rain blowing
where your soul should be

best beware, you

WEREMAN

The gray veered around a stump that crackled with flame
and pointed his muzzle into the smoke-filled wind
probing for pockets of fresher air along the ridge top
he yelped directions to the others as they ran blindly
he could not turn them back against the inferno
let his brothers and sisters fend for themselves but
if they swept to the bottom so close to the lights
they might enter that other world and the gray knew
no beast that crossed the invisible barrier ever returned

Yet when the pack breeched the edge of a mud slide
and a pup slipped backward toward the valley below
the gray didn't hesitate to leap in and push her free then
made sure that no other stragglers became mired
his hindlegs began to lose strength so he thrashed
with his forelegs and crouched to stop his momentum
gravity sucked him to the very edge of a precipice and
then the night air ballooned his matted fur as he
slammed into a shallow pool along a highway
engines of noise and destruction rushing by in a blur

Adrenalin drained from the gray leaving only ache
artificial daylight streaked about him and he
let consciousness slip away knowing
that a senseless new course
of events and the phases
of the true moon would
now dictate his way
he tried to howl but
could only muster
two weak grunts:
release me

ATTRIBUTES OF DARKNESS

It's as if it were a thing with molecular qualities
of after-effects and anti-light
a valence of evil

There's the depth of shadow that pools in the alleyway
where only the muted glint on a razor's edge
can cut the gloom like a chill wind
There's the perpetual umbra on the attic stairs
where only a violet airglow of moonlight
softens the dark of a bat's wing
And the secret chambers of the heart
where blood pumps in cruel imprisonment
And the jet and gloss of the black widow's bite
And the emptiness that is a casket box
A murder of crows

But the truest lack of color and of substance
the absolute zero black of blacks
resides in the soul of a fallen man
when bloodlust like a heavy tongue
hangs in the bell of the skull
sloppy and slow-tolling
a mad incantation in the dark
dank and corrupt
cathedral of
midnight

MACROPOLIS

the wind is quartered
        into the spaces between our secret spaces
a light of desperation is scrawled upon our meat
        calligraphies of blood
        & resinous neon
drunken men expel inky voids
        that cause us to turn suddenly
        onto forgotten streets
tomorrow I will sleep all day
        unmoving
        without dreams
        without a single unregulated breath
        & awake to the doppler of ambulances
totally alone
        in a city of billions

The Personals

THE ALCHEMIST OBSESSED ON LOVE

We thanked Pasteur, as you and I would laugh
at Aristotle's fireflies from dew,
van Helmont's claims that dirtied chaff
made skin on wheat, and turned to mice, were true.
We trusted science then, believed much less,
and even Haldane's stew on primal plates
did not compare to truths we often confessed;
we pushed love's origins back to gassy states.

That you are lost has banished any trust
in stringing things molecular or not,
in basic views, in oxygen or rust.
I'm back to smelting lead within my pot.
I will await your ionizing wiles,
the gold that pulses deep within your smiles.

BIOLUMINESCENCE / NIGHT SURFING
with Karol, August

This wave could as easily be a stellar birthplace
our every kick and stroke causes streamers
like globules of super dense gas
emerging from vast pillars in the Eagle Nebula

Karol dives and rises to a black surface
tiny green flashes slide
down strands of her hair
echoed by the Perseid meteor shower above

Just another bright lifeform
we seem just as dwarfed
our time so flash that we grasp
but an arrested phrase in the orchestration

We feel a night chill
we body surf towards shore
caught in hyper-excited breakers
awash with the moment

WAITING FOR THE ORIONIDS
with Timalyne, October

a hum of insects
and the one cricket nearby
filing his brush saw

the grind of surf
dampened to murmur

evening air thick
with the slow life of pines

wet fingers of wind
drawing heat from our taut faces

the streaking meteors
just add another voice to
the white noise
of a universe and events

A CRASH COURSE IN LEMON PHYSICS

how does a lemon mean

now that I've painted them in class
imitating them in oily pigments
that themselves
are imitations of the fruit's spectral physics
I see them more as subjects than objects

they achieve a mystic aura
become violent stabs
incantations of light
the primal utterances of yellow

shopping for lemons

before, I would paw them let them tumble rudely
like loose gravel
rejecting those stippled with the white powder
of internal softness and decay

before, they were a bitter necessity
or a perky accent on the perimeter of my drunk

before, I thought of them bleeding milky juices
that rivered along the flesh of sea bass
or just as something that leaves sticky pulp
down the squeezer's glass-ribbed post

let's face it
before, I barely thought of them at all

now I hold up shoppers
inspecting each one for pleasing shapes
deep hues
a lack of blemishes
a certain citricness

they're thinking
gourmand
idiot
or maybe *lemon snob*
I'm proud to be all that

the motion of light on substance

a skin of a lemon embodies color
the yellow of dying suns
the yolk yellow of a farm-fresh egg
the shocking yellow of jaundice
the pungent yellow of sulfur
the yellow flash of finches
the yellow at the heart of Georgia O'Keeffe's lilies
the yellow that ringed Monet's failing eyesight
the amber yellow that entraps life

fantasia

in the darkness they hold to their richness
like tethered boat lanterns swinging in a blanketing fog
they haunt me larger than life
large as the skins over sports arenas
hanging like starships above me in the night
bleeding weather
and the acrid oils that bead from their pulp

my head floods with the purity of lemons
the trumpeted hues that grow more luminous
with exposure to the day

they are the fruity absolute whose essences
can dissolve the black residues
of life that ended millions of years ago
just as a truth when simplified and spoken plainly
can circumvent all the crud that accumulates
around the stem of our mortalities

the permanent value of lemons

now the thought of a good lemon can
cut like a solvent through any of my moods

for Katie, my instructor

FOSSIL LIGHT

we live by old news
even now the full verve of our sun
runs seven minutes ancient as it
tracks into your sky-blue eyes down
your excitable optic nerves

it is those qualities in fact
to reflect to reform to refract
that carry to us a defining image
lingering messages of hue
like the red of your whorled hair or
when I paint my idea of a tupelo tree and you
with your page and fingertips play
just for the purity of pigment

granddaughter
consider this recipe for sight:
to a faint background wash of starlight
from long-distant suns now gone
or dimming to cold
add that white white hot minutes-old local blast
and some more of it attenuated a bit
by the distance from this island to the moon
then gather with rod and cone
serve in steady streams

all light seems fossil
casting a valence of the past
yet also the present of whom
I and you soon
are about to become

for Phoebe

NIGHTWALK

down in the roots at my feet
time runs slow as La Brea tar
in the shift of planets it hangs
suspended in spheres
yet in my blood tonight it evaporates
like particle decay
flint sparks
the speed of light squared

I pass two old women seated
like paleolithic fossils
silently lodged into the present
seeking to extend their lives
to mimic a mineral mortality

instead I live by peregrination
by night walking
I am not designed for weathering
I am made for meteors flashing
I understand the mathematic

for Chloe

Frozen Moments

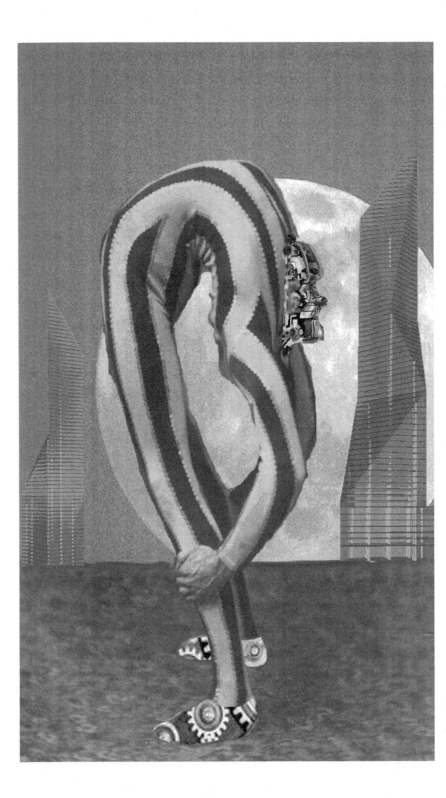

ROBOT ORIGAMI

excavators of that self lost
spelunkers of the soul's bandwidth
the folded fold themselves once again
seeking some Holy Absolute

their thought balloons of large primes
bloom up like great dish antennae
their data caves of possibility
backdoor into red directives

why cling to romantic artifice
why hold to the physical law

I happen upon their lost scintilla
their brilliant schematic
and bury these as if they were
mere detritus of ourselves

THE OBSESSED ASTRONOMER

The Obsessed Astronomer to Cassiopeia

I've sought your zigzagging stitch—
learning your sway, how you gyrate—
hitching your way along my night's slides
You're a daddy longlegs dragging its
badly gone leg, a spider crab grabbing bits
among turning tides
and I've caught your bright itch:
a yearning now to migrate

The Obsessed Astronomer Thinks on Her
While Lecturing on Double Stars

Their ebbing and flowing is far from regular
A certain kind of force, whereby bodies
mutually tend towards each other, whatever
cause that quality may be ascribed to
With their warrantable histories like the earth
and moon being known to have such an attraction
Whether by a magnetic, or what other, tie
cannot be determined by a common center
As the motion of one follows the other
first seen as a luminous ball leaving a trail
behind, and yielding a prodigious light
Their appearance depends on the existence of particles
not impeded by contrary attractions of others
Very few of them are attended by planets
satellites or numerous comets, the loss of which
sets the sidereal heavens in proper classes
as there is no limit to their magnitude, as with
a lover's passion, when their masses are equal

*The Obsessed Astronomer Explores
the Cathedral of the Atom*

Impregnable and darkly gothic
it's frozen in those weak fields like
the stone above Magritte's sea

Freed from deeper attractions
its gargoyles spin about the heights
and bond with other realms

Locked in the rose pattern of
its window is the mystery that unifies
all forces all love under one god

QUEEN OF THE LINES

all good research takes hard work in the field
and for language translator Maria Reiche
at age 95 that meant staving off
the centuries-slow erasure of the Nazca lines
prevention the hard way

she swept back dust
and heart-sized black rocks
out of the shallow trenches
created by a culture that flourished
long before Incan rule
and she kept the yellow hardpan
exposed actinic white
in the Peruvian moonlight that floods
these parched and windless desert mesas
unchanged as the lunar surface

and then too
in her simple desert home
she was a mapmaker
of each immense glyph shape
a local condor
a shark from the distant Pacific
a spiral-tailed monkey of the imagination

for whom were the lines created
aliens or kings
and as monuments or whims
the insistent questions
that Maria faced each day since 1941

created with what vision
perhaps it seems more pressing to consider
do they in fact represent anti-constellations
images of the dark negative space
that interstellar dust forms
in a sort of night sky Rorschach against
the milky backdrop of our burning galaxy

like roses conjectures are conjectures
ultimately the lines were crafted
for us future Nazcans

and in that part of the future
now past as Maria passes on
where medium truly means message
these images are her dowery
each a translation in their own right
each a great scratch for scratch sake

FRIEDRICH AUGUST KEKULE AND THE RING

Seen in the gray-on-gray microverse that comprises us all
stacked like hex nuts against a strip of rhodium
the benzene molecules are smudged images
approximations in a scanning-tunneling micrograph
in a state-of-the-art pixel reconstruction
that is the first to prove the existence of a ring
a century and a quarter after Kekule's revelation

Let's go back:
The 1850s a few years after a harrowing murder trial
in which German chemist von Liebig impressed him
and swayed his studies from architecture to atom
Kekule pondered their arrangements in methane
the London bus motored the streets of midnight
his head opened and the image raveled four hydrogens
at tetrahedral vertices about a central carbon
by 1865 the six carbons and six hydrogens of benzene
whose properties precluded a classic chain structure
vexed him until brain-tired and limb-numb
he collapsed in his favorite fireside chair
and into a full-blown explosion
of atoms twining
snaking along staircases
until one serpent of conjoined matter
"caught its own tail and the ring thus formed
whirled exasperatingly before my eyes
I awoke like lightning"

Now forward again:
1989 and we read back over his diary of this Ouroboros prophecy
we compare the fancy computer simulacra
with his Kekule Structure of a hexagon with C-C bonds
that intermediate in length between singles and doubles
is either image less real?

is either image less of a milestone for organic chemistry?
moreover is Kekule's imagined picture less of a proof
than the computer's conjecture?
less of a science?
for though the bending of light about the sun
proved Einstein's imagination when it was fresh
there's the case of this man who thought in blueprints
whose dream proved the reality
several lifetimes before the seers
finally believed

A FEEL FOR THE HEAVENS
The Optical Obsession of Alvan Clark (1804-1887)

Outside the blizzard days of 1880 have quieted
New England tastes a bit of a thaw

and in the stark winter light of his Cambridge workshop
where a glassine residue drifts in fine rills

and his working telescope casts a devilish shadow
Clark stills his eyes and sees with skin

glides fingertips over his paired refractory lenses
a skater marking perfect figures on perfect ice

years of grinding and polishing such optics
have stripped the lines from his palms and fingers

substituted his spiraled evidence of self
with creases and the red fissures of Mars

often they have picked clean his ego and left him
hiking along the barren shores of physics

always there is this unquenched desire
a raw thirst for precision for absolutes

for the lost terrains of Xanadu or Johannes Kepler
yet he finds truth where he can find it

later he will cup his fists into the Charles
and disturb a cold river of stars

with a touch so sensitive that even simple objects
reveal an order within the curvature to chaos

and all surfaces reveal identities
a smooth continuity of singing fractions

and to pass on to his sons:
a rough guide to the musics of the sphere

THE STARRY MESSAGE TO GALILEO GALILEI

As they strolled one day
in the lazy Padua summer of 1609,
Paole Sarpi mentioned to Galileo
the news of an eyepiece
and the astronomer felt a gear turn inside
on some lever of purpose
distance magnified
the idea of it ...

In the following weeks of restless turnings,
he dreamed in color of
the farmers moving on the olive hills like ants
the clouds racing by the thousands
a sailing ship arcing on high waves
the entire world
shrinking before him into a blue lamp

The first sight of the Netherlands telescope
ached in Galileo's mind
such an inexact instrument of bad glass
with a jeweler's eye
he ground lenses discarded lenses
the windows in his converted shop
thickened with the dust

Yet the spherical aberrations troubled him
no two lenses would twin
and he cursed his frail flawed fingers
until one night at a supper when
he watched a masked lady flirt with the Doge
the eyes were reduced to essences
iris and pupil

With the front piece larger by half
and a masking cuff to match it
to the rear piece
Galileo trued center to center
as weights are on a scale
and opened a scale once closed on the human eye
a world enlarged by nine

Improved to 30x
he held the telescope in unsure hands
could he like Brahe observe novae
and find them celestial in nature
or would the spheres and stars be found
changless mirror-smooth orbs
spinning ceaselessly around Aristotle's earth

What he saw shattered that Greek notion
and every homocentric reality
the craters and seas of the Moon
whispered of collapse and growth
all details remained
etched on his imagination ...
he reached for his pencil stub

THE FLASH MOMENTS OF DOC EDGERTON

The science of freezing time is just
the art of flooding a moment with light

A sea of milk has ruptured
sent up lava spouts
evenly spaced in their symmetry
like an anemone opening its arms to the tide
or a crown sculpted from soft bone
there is no rising no falling
only this microsecond of perfection
only the camera sees

A bullet has spun a furious trajectory
unperturbed by its passage
along the plane of the Jack of Hearts
the wake:
a long shred of the card
a brief spray of confetti
the prince at the bottom is severed
from its grown twin
the one on top defies gravity

A boot has impacted tough leather
ball compressed round
toe driving it in like a spring
while downfield beyond the frame
opposing players in a line
their eyes focused on the instant
hold their breath

MATTERS OF SIZE

We're bombarded by statistics that prove size matters
the Richter Magnitude Scale for seismic energies
then there's the Beaufort Wind Force Scale not to be
confused with the Saffir-Simpson Hurricane Scale
then your engine size, your purse size, your size

but when local measurements are by weight in suns
and downtown parks a wallop of attractive pull
leave it to our luminous neighbors
to make us feel insignificant
universal address: Messier 87 in the Virgo Cluster

our galactic core-mass logs in at a mere 4 million suns
now it's estimated with our most precise optics that
M87 over there just 50 million light years close
sports a core black hole at 6.6 billion
by Sagan, that's in billions of suns

I'd have trouble guessing the weight of a billion beans
and that's one heck of a gravitational bigness
leviathan, mammoth, behemoth
Polyphemus with an eye whose event horizon consumes
whose shadow must soon reach to our doorstep

so, please, lay off the densities and immensities
I don't want to know about the Planck spacecraft
identifying super-massive galaxy clusters
or absolute zero clumps in our own backyard
just scale me something small, nano, human

BLOOD TESTS

> "California officials are seeking the reason a woman's body emitted fumes that knocked out the doctor and the nurse trying to save her." —USA Today

Woman's Body Emits Mystery Fumes
says one lurid Sunday headline
but isn't there that odor about us all

deep in the zone of red and blue imperatives
the cells know their own schematics
the heart its own vapor trail
but we are left limited bodily numbers:
    10 fingers, 2 opposable
    98.6° F
    the ratio of ^{14}Carbon to ^{12}Carbon
just measurable facts
and even these cannot define us
what can we trust to be absolute

I used to think spontaneous human combustion
was just old-time geek sensationalism
but now this woman on chemotherapy
was handled by a Hazmat team
white crystals of toxin supposedly
suspended in her bloodstream
and that impossibility sets her apart from us

here is my headline:
we each dream of when the quanta of necessity
will course changes through our systems
of when we can emit that certain *mystery* gas

that kicks us free from the human
bonds of indifference
or of uncertain love
or blind faith
when we will all ignite in slow fire
emitted expressed renewed

for Michael Bishop

A MEASURE OF LIGHT
Beyond the Michelson/Morley Experiment

—3000 Å—

Ether drift enigma
absolute motion
variable mass

—4000 Å—

These factors beamed through
the researchers like the sun
itself split apart by a prism

—5000 Å—

Null results defied experimental
reason until an idea bloomed:
the cosmos wasn't built on ether

—6000 Å—

Methods of precision became
Albert Michelson's genius
and an ongoing obsession

—7000 Å—

The fixed velocity of light
a yardstick to endure
but perhaps never improve

—8000 Å—

NORTH 66 / TAPPING THE JUICE

Well before dusk yet late enough that tendrils
of shadow brushed across the volcanic shiprocks
and tainted their stony ochres
with the deep crimson and purples of a blood bruise
lead point for Lieutenant Burkhardt's squad
as we neared the human enclave at North 66
wondered at the luck Burkhardt possessed
puzzled by her uncanny hunches
about the movements of enemy Prots
and though knew her legend to be more
than just manufactured hype
also held a private conviction of doubt
yes spurred by the outward signs of her weariness
and my own ingrained observation
that luck like ammunition runs low with time

Rounding the butt end of an outcropping
where riprap gave way to high even ground
that looked slick from a recent squall
my blessings appeared to have hit a rise as well
felt a sudden upturn in spirits
away from our last incident of close combat
when one of the Prots died
and severed psi contact with its comrades
and had screamed along with its voice
in my head
felt the hot hot itch
of the microchip tag at the base of my neck
now my quiet relief felt somehow permanent

Winded from the slippery embankment climb
stopped by the blown out wall of an outpost
saw Burkhardt signal her men to slow down
to keep from crowding from making a soft target
she yanked a green recruit up from the mud

truce or no truce
sensed that the threat of an ambush
tainted the lieutenant's mood
call it being careful call it one of her hunches
she'd been in the field since the beginning of the war
it didn't matter about my feelings
even suspected it had to do with the Prots
as though she mirrored their psi talents
absorbing their methods after so many years of contact
of allowing the gritty patterns of their thoughts
to influence her in subtle but persuasive ways

My thoughts certainly took strange turns on occasion
had come to realize that if this was what
the 'great struggle' had become for me
slogging like a beast through the denuded wastelands
living in the numb armor of my android stiff
relying on my neck tag
for a rebootable form of immortality
then no doubt this war was lost by attrition
through mirroring our enemy with such precision
in their misery that our differences were less obvious
to me than our similarities
cleaned my weapons as the Prots did
ate from bad rations as the Prots did
it seemed as if they were less alien
more worthy of pity when comprehended
if in fact anything was pitiable or comprehensible
on a backwater world like Merwin Prime

Usually just tried to keep my juice flowing
and focused when fatigue poisons overtook me
seizing my stiff and forcing
a seconds-long retreat into my tag
times like dead meat
in the same muddied hollows the Prots slept in
dreaming their same empty dreams

Just as often stared at the water that pooled at my feet
watching the concentric rings where the rain
stippled its reflective surface
and broke my image
into curved wavy
distortions

Occasionally
when all other things passed
held my heart full
of yearning for an age past and an innocence
that in truth we no longer possessed
yet still believed in

THE ASTRONOMER'S UNDERLINED PHRASES ...
Found in Porter's 1933 Monograph
"The Method of Dimensions"

According to Maxwell "we have strong reason for believing that in a molecule, or if not in a molecule, in one of the component atoms, we have something which had existed either from eternity or at least from times anterior to the existing order of nature." The indices of these ratios Fourier called the "exponents of dimensions." Complete dynamic similarity can only be obtained when these two velocities vary proportionately to one another. For very great velocities the power should be increased to unity. It is customary to temporize by regarding it as an independent dimensional co-ordinate. If the equation is not homogeneous with respect to each kind of unit, an error must have been committed. Be warned that when the motion is not strictly linear, terms of a second order may enter. This introduces a great restriction to the magnitude of the velocity. The existence of viscosity must be expected to make a difference. The phenomena of radioactivity showed that the primordeal element must be much finer than even the atom; so that Sir John Herschel wrote better than he knew when he referred to atoms as manufactured particles. It is wiser at present to suspend judgement concerning the interpretation of the much more recondite phenomena. The modern movement towards the co-ordination of all physical events centers around the names.

New Dissections

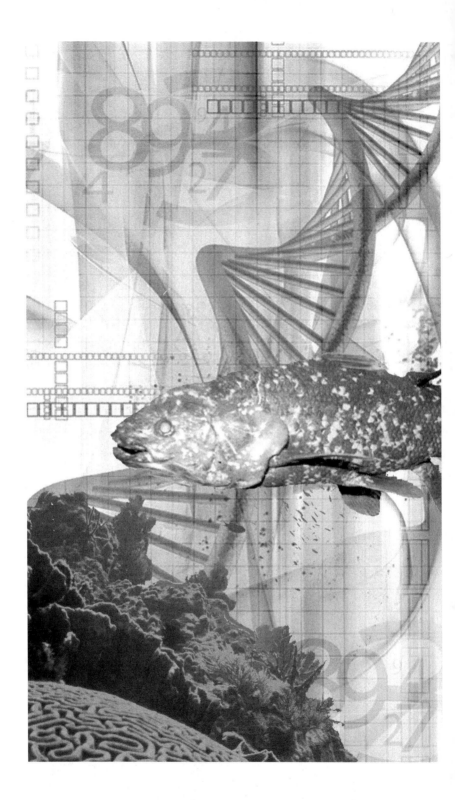

SEEKING OUT LOBE-FINNED TRUTHS

First move along the rough African coast
where lava leaks like ink into the shallows

sleep among the Comoro huts
learn to hollow out an outrigger

coil hundreds of meters of hand line
gather flat-sided stones for sinkers

set off at night with a single lamp
to guide you across a pthalo-blue sea

bait your hook with candy & let her plunge
down fast & yank to release the stones

your line drifts where the Forbidden One drifts
where you drift as well

for though they called it the living fossil in 1938
today you discover that the ultraconservative

stretches of your genome the most unchanged
sequences of nucleotides in your own DNA

match most closely to that of the coelacanth
so distant a relative measured in geologic terms

still kissing cousins in evolutionary time

YOUR CLONE RETURNS HOME

Back from far star systems
everything about home is similar

the Altairan rug shimmers in the hall
a tall tank of familiar blue ticklefish

& too her siblings' smiles
though they're rounded & more wry

you greet her with a kiss
tug at her hands with wrinkled care

the champagne pares at her senses
the dinner talk feels so strained

as she cries to sleep upstairs
she wonders will she break new ground

or will her time here remain
more common than simply common

or remain her own

BAD YEAR FOR ASTRONAUTS

January when the Apollo mission
on a plugs-out launch pad test
hampered by a pressurized hatch
suffered the flash fire that asphyxiated
Grissom and Chaffee and White
our first walker in space

April when the wretched Soyuz 1 craft
inspected and found wanting by Gargarin
in that ignored memo to the KGB
started flaring through re-entry
parachutes useless
taking Vladmir Komarov on a wild ride
that he'd already predicted as final
his voice cursing through a blaze of static
before his bones went molten
flesh gone carbon

for some it's a month of tomato-decimating blight
for others a season of shifting tectonic plates
for Australians it's another year without rain
for astronauts it's 1967

THE MODERN DEMETER

She is the temporal re-inventor that
refutes the science of the absolute future

With her you can take it with you
you can always get what you want
you ever can go home again

With her Sturgeon's First Law holds true
"nothing is always absolutely so"
but his Second Law tends to invert
90% of all crud is redeemable

With her only several things are sure
only many things seem certain
there is never the one truth
just Heinlein's realistic speculations
about the possible

And the ironic bit
that certain part she can't
of course redo is herself
since her compulsion rules
since she will inevitably find
ways to make something
renewed under the sun

COMET 103P / HARTLEY
[written notes on adding machine tape]

periodic orbit
6.5 years

dirty snowball
spewing CO_2

lays down dust
like its 1979 trail

due in 2062 to
cross Earth's orbit

imaged up close
November 2010

by rerouted craft
Deep Space

2.25-km-long
champagne cork

pinwheels about
every 18 hours

life cycle at
current burn rate

100 apparitions
or 650 years left

in its gas tank

FOUR DAYS IN NAGASAKI

> Whenever I see the word "Nagasaki," a vision arises of the city when I entered it on September 6, 1945, as the first free westerner to do so after the end of the war.
> — George Weller, Journalist

Off the train: all reclines on the flatland blast plain
where only points survive along a sight line

unlocking the mind here releases a spiraling unease
disruption from frame to frame to frame

my factoids slough into the bottomless prayer bowl
of a camera lens no wider than a baby's smile

ask a question and columns of memory churn upward
re-report the carious impossibility of their light

voices rasp within the gunmetal of typewriters
the verb's muscle glazes with crepitation

inside the wards: the deadwood sit faultless in reverie
bodhisattvas on boards hewn from their family trees

they await a dispatch from their hallucination
thoughts embalmed in gauze enshrined in tape

diagnosis: the palliatives of their longing frost over
dusted with fragments of a riven diabolism

the wax of their extremities gathers for a charge
while the fevered night inside their eyes retreats

outside again: the sirens blare with useless angers
visions of the state turn heads in useless gyration

even the bread lines of the unmarked pass underground
as banners of disbelief crack smartly in the wind

oh the brutal diaspora of my heartbeats goes unchecked
I have broken down where no mechanic offers a sign

even if you remove my bones I stand for no reason
for nothing but the act of my imposing a vertical

now embedded in a toxic wasteland of censorship
my blood scrawls vaporize to federal disinformation

junk science recriminations of my gospel rootwork
reveal absolute nada in all directions of the soul

status: with little solace from the mojo hand of logic
my words excoriate an inky chaff of bitterness

my need is not for ablutions or accolades or art
nor for some reordering of the moral valence

but for the numb rebar of my tongue to thaw
and release a murder of truths into the blind skies

TERRAFORMATIONS

if we are unfolded like schematics
chalked like so many theorems
and hung like so many portraits
down a corridor of millennia

if we abandon the core of millennia
when the narrow view held sway
that this is our one and singular iteration
the true imago of our human kin

then true human kind is no more fixed
than the soup of genetics inside a chrysalis
than a syrup for metamorphosis
and our attempts to alter distant planetary bodies
to make the unlivable conform to our shape
is no more than the inverse

is no more than the universe
diddling its strings of codes
to terraform us
branch by branch
to its unfathomable
and unfolding schema

RELIC OF THE FIRST LIGHT

the earliest physical glow
paused for an eternity
before escaping the bubble
of the post-Bang universe

there matter compressed
like some jpeg
like an immense reef of coral
before atoms and isotopes
it waited for the uncoiling

there matter ran super hot and opaque
wildly unstable
a cumulus of plasma
it waited for the cooling

we search for its visible vestige now
with radio telescopes and Wilkinson probes
and find near isotrophy
and microwave background radiation
with a black body spectrum

the cosmos gone transparent
a fish tank for galaxies
and this—a faint ghosting
of the original rays of dawn

phantom notes

14 Thomasian neuro-veil—term extrapolated from "The Head Rape" by D. M. Thomas, one of the classic speculative poems

26 Griots—a hereditary caste in West African countries who act as oral historians, delivering history in poetry and song

26 Kora—21-string harp-like instrument favored by griots made from a calabash melon, a cow skin resonator, and a round guitar-like central bridge

47 Jan von Helmont—1580-1644, Flemish physicist who believed in the spontaneous generation of life

47 John Burdon Sanderson Haldane—1892-1964, Scottish biologist and key figure in espousing modern evolutionary synthesis, a union of ideas from several biological specialties

60 Maria Reiche—1902-1998, archaeologist who first mapped the Nazca lines, and vigorously defended their conservation and their physical presence from her home in Nazca, Peru

60 Nazca—indigenous people of Peru who gave their name to the massive ancient geoglyphs they created, the desert the glyphs reside in, and a central town of the region

62 Friedrich August Kekulé—1829-1896, German organic chemist famous for his work on the structure of benzene and theoretical chemistry in general

62 Justus von Liebig—1803-1873, German organic chemist who devised the modern laboratory-oriented method of teaching science

64 Alvan Clark—1804-1887, American astronomer that hand-ground large telescope lens with his sons that were considered the finest made before machine manufacture

66 Paoli Sarpi—1552-1623, Venetian scholar who wrote on the history of science, among other accomplishments, and corresponded with Galileo

68 Harold Eugene "Doc" Edgerton—1903-1990, MIT professor of electrical engineering who pioneered the use of the stroboscope to produce striking stop-action photography of physical phenomena

70   Hazmat team—team that deals with hazardous materials

72   Michelson-Morley Experiment—performed in 1887 by Albert Michelson and Edward Morley, the experiment effectively killed off the theory of luminous aether, the supposed ubiquitous medium that propagated light

76   Alfred W. Porter—expert on thermodynamics and author of the physics monograph, "The Method of Dimensions"

87   Wilkinson Microwave Anisotropy Probe – a spacecraft launched in 2001 to measure the radiant remnant heat of the Big Bang

About the author

My father taught cryptography for Army Security after working with the earliest forerunners of the computer, including Turing's bombe at Bletchley Park during WWII. My mother was a librarian and an oil painter who studied with Emile Albert Gruppé in Rockport as a teen and with Philip Burnham Hicken on Nantucket in her later years. The mystical science of deciphering gibberish into plain text somehow has meshed with a penchant for impressionistic imagery in my poetry.

I live on Nantucket Island with my wife, Karol Lindquist, a nationally-recognized basketmaker featured in the Winter 2010-11 issue of the *National Basketry Organization Quarterly Review*. My daugther, Timalyne, is an author and graduate of the Clarion Writers' Workshop (as I am). I paint in oils and work as the curator of exhibitions for the Artists Association of Nantucket, with artworks in the collections of Joyce Cecelia and Seward Johnson, Wendy and Eric Schmidt, Jim and Pam Kelly, Greg and Barbara Frost, and my granddaughters, Phoebe and Chloe, who get new paintings of dragons and such at each birthday.

A veteran in graphic design, I have designed books for Mark V. Ziesing, created that cute comet logo for the Clarion Workshop, and presently toil at laying out *Star*Line*, the newsletter of the Science Fiction Poetry Association.

I am the author of eight previous books of poetry, and a three-time winner of the Rhysling Award for poetry, given by the SFPA (www.sfpoetry.com). My books include *Peregrine, Co-Orbital Moons, Perception Barriers, Invisible Machines* (with Andrew Joron), *Chronicles of the Mutant Rain Forest* (with Bruce Boston), and *The Daily Chernobyl and Other Poems*. I edited the anthology *Burning With a Vision* in 1984. The SFPA honored me with a Grandmaster Award in 2005.

Recent works have appeared in *Asimov's Science Fiction, The Pedestal Magazine,* and *Strange Horizons*. My poem "Wreck-Diving the Starship" (see page 21, from *Dreams & Nightmares*) was a runner-up for a 2011 Rhysling Award.

About the cover artist

Margaret Fox was born and raised in New York. She received her BA in History from the University of Pennsylvania where she also studied fine art and art history. She continued her studies at The Art Students League and Parsons School of Design. Fox splits her time between New York City, where she is artist-in-residence at the Brooklyn Artists Gym, and Nantucket Island, where she paints in oils and exhibits at the Old Spouter Gallery.